CURRIES

Distributed in Australia & New Zealand by BONZA Books a division of
R&R Publications Marketing Pty. Ltd. (ACN 083 612 579)
12 Edward Street, Brunswick, Victoria 3056
Australia-wide toll Free 1800 063 296

Photographs and recipes by Rolli Books
Typeset by MATS, Southend-on-Sea, Essex
Printed in Slovenia
Designed and created by Consortium, England
production co-ordination by Daphne Wannee, Rebo International
Edited by Anne Sheasby
Illustrations by Camilla Sopwith

J0249AUS

ISBN 1 740220 00 5

CURRIES

FRAGRANT AND SPICY DISHES

FROM EXCITING EVERYDAY MEALS TO EXCOTIC ENTERTAINING

Contents

Introduction

Curry originates from the Indian subcontinent, but contrary to popular belief, not all Indian food is 'curry'. It is the sauce, containing an intricate combination of herbs and spices cooked to make an aromatic base for a variety of dishes, that constitutes curry.

The extensive range of spices available offers a feast of diverse flavours to complement and enhance chicken and lamb, fish and seafood, vegetables and vegetarian-based dishes.

Not all curries are chilli-hot. In this book, we offer a collection of recipes for authentic curries that vary in character from the mildly aromatic and rich and creamy to the pungently spiced and fiery hot. Any one of the hotter curries can be made milder by simply reducing the amount of chillies used without adversely affecting the essential flavour of the dish.

Basic Curry Recipes

Many of the following are used as components in recipes throughout the book.

Paneer

In a saucepan, bring 3 litres (5¼ pints) of milk to the boil. Just before the milk boils, add 90 ml (6 tbsp) of lemon juice or vinegar to curdle the milk. Strain the curdled milk through a piece of muslin to allow all the whey and moisture to drain away. Still wrapped in the muslin, place the paneer under a weight and refrigerate for 2-3 hours to allow it to set into a block. The paneer can then be cut or grated from the block.

Garlic paste and ginger paste

Soak 300 g (10½ oz) of fresh ginger or garlic cloves overnight to soften the skins. Peel and chop roughly. Process in a food processor, or pound with a pestle and mortar, until pulped. The pulp can be stored in an airtight container and refrigerated for 4-6 weeks.

Onion paste

Peel and chop 500 g (1 lb 2 oz) onions into quarters. Process in a food processor, or pound with a pestle and mortar, until pulped. Refrigerate in an airtight container for 4-6 weeks.

Cashew nut and almond paste

Process 300 g (10½ oz) of blanched almonds or raw cashew nuts in a food processor, or pound with a pestle and mortar, with enough groundnut or vegetable oil to form a thick paste. Process or pound until fairly smooth. Refrigerate in an airtight container.

Green chilli or red chilli paste

Roughly chop the required amount of green or red chillies, and process in a food processor, or pound with a pestle and mortar, until pulped.

Coconut paste

Crack open a fresh coconut, reserving the coconut milk, and break in half. Carefully remove the coconut flesh from the hard shell with a knife and break into 2.5-cm (1-in) pieces. Process in a food processor with a little coconut milk, or pound with a pestle and mortar, until pulped.

Poppy seed paste

Process poppy seeds in a food processor, or pound with a pestle and mortar, with enough vegetable oil to form a paste.

Garam masala

Garam masala is widely available as a ready-prepared spice mix, but it is easy to make your own mix and is likely to be fresher and more aromatic than the shop-bought variety.

Finely grind together the following ingredients: 90 g (3¼ oz) cumin seeds, 70 g (2½ oz) black peppercorns, 75 g (2¾ oz) black cardamom seeds, 25 g (1 oz) fennel seeds, 40 g (1½ oz) green cardamoms, 35 g (1¼ oz) coriander seeds, 20 g (¾ oz) cloves, 20 cinnamon sticks, 2.5 cm (1 in) in length, 20 g (¾ oz) ground mace, 20 g (¾ oz) black cumin seeds, 15 g (½ oz). dried rose petals, 15 g (½ oz) dried bay leaves, 15 g (½ oz) ground ginger. Store in an airtight container in a cool, dry place.

Pot Cooked Chicken

This is a delectable yet easy to make one-pot chicken curry.

Preparation time: 30 minutes • Cooking time: 45 minutes • Serves: 4

Ingredients

800 g (1 lb 12 oz) boneless chicken thighs	*10 cloves*
A pinch of saffron	*4 cardamoms*
75 ml (5 tbsp) vegetable oil	*20 ml (4 tsp) ginger paste* *(page 7)*
25 g (1 oz) garlic, chopped	*20 ml (4 tsp) garlic paste* *(page 7)*
90 g (3¼ oz) onions, sliced	*Salt, to taste*
2.5-cm (1-inch) piece of cinnamon stick	*2.5 ml (½ tsp) yellow or red chilli powder*
	500 ml (18 fl oz) chicken stock

Method

1
Cut the chicken into bite-sized pieces.

2
Soak the saffron in a little water in a small bowl for 10 minutes. Drain and set aside.

3
Meanwhile, heat the oil in a saucepan and add the chopped garlic. Cook until brown.

4
Add the onions and cook until slightly browned, stirring occasionally.

5
Add the cinnamon, cloves and cardamoms and cook until the onions turn golden brown.

6
Add the ginger and garlic pastes, chicken, salt and yellow or red chilli powder. Stir for 3-4 minutes.

7
Add the chicken stock and bring to the boil. Cover and simmer for about 30 minutes or until the chicken is cooked and tender.

8
Remove the pan from the heat. Remove the chicken using a slotted spoon and keep hot. Strain the juices, discarding any pulp.

9
Return the juices to the pan, bring to the boil and boil rapidly until the sauce is thickened and reduced.
Add the chicken and reheat thoroughly. Stir in the prepared saffron and serve.

Serving suggestion
Serve hot with an Indian bread of your choice.

Variation
Use half white or red wine and half stock in place of all stock, for a richer flavour.

Chicken Stuffed with Nuts

A rich and creamy dish, known in India as Murgh Musallam.

Preparation time: 25 minutes • Cooking time: 1 hour • Serves: 4

Ingredients

One 900 g (2 lb) chicken, skinned
100 ml (3½ fl oz) vegetable oil
8 cardamoms
10 ml (2 tsp) fennel seeds
4 cinnamon sticks
10 cloves
150 g (5½ oz) onion paste (page 9)
10 ml (2 tsp) red chilli powder
5 ml (1 tsp) ground black pepper
Salt, to taste
10 ml (2 tsp) ground coriander
15 ml (1 tbsp) poppy seed paste ((page 9)
15 ml (1 tbsp) almond paste (page 9)
150 g (5½ oz) fresh coconut paste (page 9)
400 ml (14 fl oz) hot water
A pinch of saffron
30 ml (2 tbsp) double cream
2.5 ml (½ tsp) ground nutmeg
2 drops almond essence
25 g (1 oz) flaked almonds, toasted, to garnish
10 ml (2 tsp) fresh coriander, chopped, to garnish

For the stuffing

800 g (1lb 12 oz) chicken mince
100 g (3½ oz) almonds, blanched
25 g (1 oz) pistachio nuts, chopped
15 ml (1 tbsp) raisins
45 ml (3 tbsp) brandy (optional)
20 ml (4 tsp) double cream
5 ml (1 tsp) ginger paste (page 7)
5 ml (1 tsp) green chilli paste (page 9)
2.5 ml (½ tsp) ground mace
Salt, to taste

Method

1
In a bowl, combine all the ingredients for the stuffing and mix well. Spoon it into the stomach cavity of the chicken.

2
In a pan, heat the oil and fry the stuffed chicken until it is golden brown all over. Set aside.

3
In the same pan, add the cardamoms, fennel seeds, cinnamon sticks, cloves and onion paste. Cook for 30-60 seconds. Add the red chilli powder, black pepper, salt and ground coriander. Cook over a low heat for 5-10 minutes.

4
Add the poppy seed, almond and coconut pastes and the hot water and bring to the boil.

5
Add the chicken, cover and cook over a low heat for about 45 minutes until the chicken is cooked and tender, stirring occasionally.

6
Remove the chicken from the pan and strain the sauce. Add the saffron, cream, nutmeg and almond essence to the sauce and mix well.

7
Place the chicken on a serving platter. Pour the sauce over the chicken and garnish with flaked almonds and fresh coriander.

Serving suggestion

Serve with Indian bread such as naan or paratha.

Cook's tip

To toast flaked almonds, spread a thin layer over a baking sheet and toast under a medium/hot grill until lightly browned. Cool and use as required.

Murgh Kastoori

As with almost every fenugreek delicacy, this dish tastes best made with fresh fenugreek, if you can obtain it.

Preparation time: 45 minutes • Cooking time: 50 minutes • Serves: 4

Ingredients

1 kg (2 lb 4 oz) boneless chicken
225 g (8 z) plain yogurt
Salt, to taste
150 ml (1/4 pint) vegetable oil
10 cardamoms
2 black cardamoms
8 cloves
2 cinnamon sticks
2 bay leaves
2.5 ml (1/2 tsp) black cumin
25 g (1 oz) onions, chopped
25 g (1 oz) garlic, chopped
55 g (2 oz) root ginger, peeled and chopped
15 ml (1 tbsp) green chillies, slit, seeded and chopped
5 ml (1 tsp) ground turmeric
7.5 ml (1 1/2 tsp) ground coriander
7.5 ml (1 1/2 tsp) red chilli powder
175 g (6 oz) tomatoes, skinned and chopped
15 ml (1 tbsp) ground fenugreek, or 200 g (7 oz) fresh fenugreek
5 ml (1 tsp) ground mace
10 ml (2 tsp) garam masala *(page 9)*
10 ml (2 tsp) ginger juliennes
15 ml (1 tbsp) fresh coriander, chopped, plus extra for garnishing

Method

1
Cut the chicken into 15 pieces, skin and set aside.

2
Whisk the yogurt in a large bowl, add the chicken and salt and stir to mix. Marinate the chicken in the yogurt mixture for at least 30 minutes.

3
Heat the oil in a heavy-based pan. Add the whole spices (cardamoms, cloves, cinnamon sticks and bay leaves) and cook over a medium heat for a few minutes.

4
Add the black cumin and onions and cook until golden brown. Add the garlic, ginger and green chillies and stir-fry for 2 minutes. Add the turmeric, coriander and red chilli powder and stir to mix.

5
Add 60 ml (4 tbsp) water and stir-fry for 30 seconds. Add the tomatoes and cook over a medium heat until the oil separates from the mixture.

6
Add the marinated chicken along with the marinade and 175 ml (6 fl oz) water. Bring to the boil, cover and simmer for about 30 minutes, until the chicken is cooked and tender and the oil separates from the sauce once again. Adjust the seasoning.

7
Sprinkle the ground fenugreek, mace, garam masala, ginger juliennes and fresh coriander over the chicken mixture. (If using fresh fenugreek, chop and cook it with the chicken.) Cover and cook for a further 5 minutes.

8
Serve hot, garnished with fresh coriander.

Serving suggestion

Serve with boiled or plain rice, or Indian bread.

Variation

Use lamb or pork in place of chicken.

Chicken Shahjahani

A chicken recipe from the kitchens of the Mughal emperors.

Preparation time: 15 minutes • Cooking time: 35 minutes • Serves: 4

Ingredients

75 ml (5 tbsp) vegetable oil
2 bay leaves
3 cinnamon sticks
8 cardamoms
2.5 ml (½ tsp) ground black cumin
8 cloves
200 g (7 oz) onions, chopped
5 ml (1 tsp) ground turmeric
10 ml (2 tsp) yellow or red chilli powder
25 g (1 oz) ginger paste *(page 7)*
25 g (1 oz) garlic paste *(page 7)*
100 g (3½ oz) cashew nut paste *(page 9)*
One 1 kg (2lb 4 oz) chicken, skinned and cut into 8 pieces
150 g (¼ pint) plain yogurt
400 ml (14 fl oz) hot water
Salt, to taste
45 ml (3 tbsp) double cream
2.5 ml (½ tsp) ground black cardamom

To garnish

3 eggs, hard boiled and quartered
15 ml (1 tbsp) fresh coriander, chopped
5 ml (1 tsp) ginger juliennes
½ red pepper, cut into strips

Method

1
Heat the oil in a heavy-based saucepan over a medium heat. Add the bay leaves, cinnamon sticks, cardamoms, black cumin and cloves and cook until the spices begin to crackle.

2
Add the onions, turmeric and yellow or red chilli powder and cook for 30 seconds.

3
Add the ginger, garlic and cashew nut pastes and cook for a further 30 seconds.

4
Add the chicken pieces and cook for 10-15 minutes over a medium heat, stirring occasionally.

5
Add the yogurt with the hot water and salt. Cover and simmer for 10-15 minutes on a very low heat, stirring occasionally.

6
Stir in the cream and ground cardamom. Garnish with hard-boiled eggs, fresh coriander, ginger juliennes and red pepper strips and serve.

Serving suggestion

Serve on a bed of boiled rice, accompanied by raita (plain yogurt mixed with some lightly crushed, dry-fried cumin seeds and sprinkled with a little red chilli powder).

Creamy Chicken Curry

A dish of mild, fragrantly-spiced chicken in a rich cream and yogurt sauce.

Preparation time: 30 minutes • Cooking time: 35 minutes • Serves: 4

Ingredients

One 1 kg (2lb 4 oz) chicken
7.5 ml (5 tbsp) vegetable oil
2 bay leaves
3 cinnamon sticks
8 cardamoms
8 cloves
200 g (7 oz) onions, chopped
5 ml (1 tsp) ground turmeric
7.5 ml (1½ tsp) red chilli powder
25 g (1 oz) ginger paste (page 7)
25 g (1 oz) garlic paste (page 7)
100 g (3½ oz) cashew nut paste (page 9)
15 ml (1 tbsp) salt
150 g (5½ oz) plain yogurt
75 ml (5 tbsp) double cream
15 ml (1 tbsp) garam masala (page 9)
2.5 ml (½ tsp) ground fenugreek
15 ml (1 tbsp) chopped fresh coriander, to garnish

Method

1
Clean and skin the chicken. Cut it into 8 pieces.

2
Heat the oil in a heavy-based pan over a medium heat. Add the bay leaves, cinnamon sticks, cardamoms and cloves and cook until they begin to crackle.

3
Add the chopped onions, turmeric and red chilli powder and cook for a further 30 seconds.

4
Add the ginger, garlic and cashew nut pastes and cook for a further 30 seconds.

5
Add the chicken pieces, stir and cook for 10-15 minutes over a medium heat.

6
Add the salt, yogurt and 30 ml (2 tbsp) hot water. Cover and simmer for 10 minutes over a low heat. Add the cream, garam masala and fenugreek. Continue to cook for 2-3 minutes, stirring.

7
To serve, transfer the chicken to a serving platter and garnish with the fresh coriander.

Serving suggestion

Serve with stir-fried okra and basmati rice.

Fried Chicken Curry

A classic curry dish of boneless chicken pieces simmered in a spicy gravy.

Preparation time: 20 minutes • Cooking time: 45 minutes • Serves: 4

Ingredients

One 1.25 kg (2lb 12 oz) chicken
2.5 ml (½ tsp) red chilli powder
5 ml (1 tsp) ground turmeric
Salt, to taste
45 ml (3 tbsp) ginger paste (page 7)
30 ml (2 tbsp) garlic paste (page 7)
75 ml (5 tbsp) groundnut oil
25 g (1 oz) tamarind
12 curry leaves
85 g (3 oz) onions, chopped
125 g (4½ oz) tomatoes, skinned and chopped
2.5 ml (½ tsp) ground cardamom
2.5 ml (½ tsp) ground coriander
1.25 ml (¼ tsp) ground cloves
1.25 ml (¼ tsp) ground cinnamon
2.5 ml (½ tsp) black peppercorns, crushed
15 ml (1 tbsp) lemon juice
20 ml (4 tsp) chopped fresh coriander leaves, to garnish

Method

1
Clean the chicken. Debone, skin and cut the meat into 4-cm (1½-in) cubes.

2
Mix the red chilli powder, turmeric and salt with half the ginger and garlic pastes. Rub this marinade on to the chicken pieces. Cover and set aside for 30 minutes.

3
Heat the oil in a wok (kadhai), add the marinated chicken and cook over a medium heat until lightly browned all over. Remove the chicken and reserve the oil.

4
Soak the tamarind in 25 ml (5 tsp) water. After 10 minutes, mash well, squeeze out the pulp and discard. Set the juice extract aside.

5
Reheat the reserved oil, add the curry leaves and cook over a low heat for 30 seconds. Add the onions and cook until lightly browned.

6
Add the remaining ginger and garlic pastes. Stir for 1 minute, then add the tomatoes and stir again. Cook until the fat appears on the sides of the pan. Add the cardamom, ground coriander, cloves and cinnamon and stir for 1 minute. Add the tamarind and cook for 5 minutes, stirring occasionally.

7
Add the chicken pieces and simmer for 8-10 minutes. Add 250 ml (9 fl oz) water and bring to the boil. Reduce to a medium heat and cook, stirring constantly, until the moisture has evaporated and the sauce coats the chicken pieces.

8
Sprinkle with pepper and lemon juice. Transfer to a serving dish and garnish with fresh coriander.

Serving suggestion

Serve with Indian bread, such as paratha.

Variation

Use red onions or shallots in place of standard onions.

Pepper Chicken

A southern Indian chicken delicacy with black peppercorns, which give the dish a special, delicious flavour.

Preparation time: 25 minutes, plus 30 minutes marinating time • Cooking time: 45 mintues • Serves: 4

Ingredients

One 1.25 kg (2 lb 12 oz) chicken

20 ml (4 tsp) black peppercorns

125 g (4½ oz) plain yogurt

45 ml (3 tbsp) ginger paste *(page 7)*

45 ml (3 tbsp) garlic paste *(page 7)*

30 ml (2 tbsp) lemon juice

Salt, to taste

60 ml (4 tbsp) groundnut oil

175 g (6 oz) onions, chopped

175 g (6 oz) tomatoes, skinned and chopped

5 ml (1 tsp) garam masala *(page 9)*

Curry leaves or chopped fresh coriander, to garnish

Method

1
Clean and cut the chicken into 8 pieces.

2
Crush the peppercorns with a pestle and mortar to form a powder.

3
Whisk the yogurt and add the ground peppercorns, half the ginger and garlic pastes, lemon juice and salt. Mix well.

4
Add the chicken pieces, stir to mix and set aside to marinate for at least 30 minutes.

5
Meanwhile, heat the oil in a wok (kadhai). Add the onions and cook over a medium heat until lightly browned.

6
Add the remaining ginger and garlic pastes and cook until the onions are golden brown, stirring occasionally.

7
Add the tomatoes and stir-fry until the fat appears on the sides of the pan.

8
Add the chicken along with the marinade and stir-fry for 4-5 minutes. Add 250 ml (9 fl oz) water and bring to the boil.

9
Cover and simmer, stirring occasionally, until the chicken is cooked and tender.

10
Adjust the seasoning. Sprinkle the garam masala over the top and stir to mix.
Garnish with curry leaves or fresh coriander and serve.

Serving suggestion
Serve with chapattis or boiled rice.

Variation
Use lime juice in place of the lemon juice and add some finely grated zest for a sharper flavour.

Butter Chicken

A rich roast chicken delicacy which is a favourite in the north of India. Use ready-made tandoori chicken available from supermarkets or Indian stores.

Preparation time: 20 minutes • Cooking time: 30 minutes • Serves: 4

Ingredients

125 g (4½ oz) butter

2 cinnamon sticks

10 cardamoms

1 bay leaf

55 g (2 oz) ginger paste (page 7)

55 g (2 oz) garlic paste (page 7)

900 g (2 lb) tomatoes, skinned and chopped

Salt, to taste

10 ml (2 tsp) ginger juliennes

5 green chillies, slit and seeded

5 ml (1 tsp) paprika

600 g (1 lb 4 oz) tandoori chicken

150 ml (¼ pint) double cream

15 ml (1 tbsp) honey

15 ml (1 tbsp) chopped fresh coriander, to garnish

Method

1
Melt half the butter in a heavy-based saucepan. Add the cinnamon, cardamoms and bay leaf and cook for 30 seconds. Stir in the ginger and garlic pastes and cook until the juices evaporate.

2
Add the tomatoes and salt and cook until the tomatoes are pulped. Add 400 ml (14 fl oz) water, bring to the boil and simmer for 20 minutes.

3
Strain the juices through a sieve into another pan.

4
Melt the remaining butter in a wok (kadhai). Add the ginger juliennes and green chillies and cook for 1 minute.

5
Add the paprika – the colour of the mixture will turn a bright red. Add the strained juices and bring to the boil.

6
Add the tandoori chicken pieces and simmer for 10 minutes until the chicken is thoroughly heated through. Stir in the cream and honey and serve garnished with fresh coriander.

Serving suggestion
Serve with any Indian breads.

Chicken Badam Pasanda

This is a light, mild curry dish – succulent chicken steaks served in an almond-yogurt sauce.

Preparation time: 20 minutes, plus 1 hour marinating time • Cooking time: 30 minutes • Serves: 4

Ingredients

100 g (3½ oz) clarified butter or ghee
25 g (1 oz) almonds, blanched and sliced
8 boneless, skinless chicken breasts
55 g (2 oz) ginger paste *(page 7)*
250 g (9 oz) plain yogurt
55 g (2 oz) garlic paste *(page 7)*
Salt, to taste
10 cardamoms
10 cloves
100 g (3½ oz) onions, chopped
250 g (9 oz) tomatoes, skinned and chopped
5 ml (1 tsp) red chilli powder
10 ml (2 tsp) plain flour
2.5 ml (½ tsp) ground black pepper
1 litre (1¾ pints) chicken stock
2.5 ml (½ tsp) ground mace
A pinch of saffron, dissolved in 15 ml (1 tbsp) milk
20 ml (4 tsp) chopped fresh coriander, to garnish

Method

1
Heat 15 g (½ oz) of the clarified butter or ghee in a frying pan. Add the almonds and brown all over. Remove the pan from the heat and set aside.

2
Clean and flatten the chicken breasts until about 1 cm (½ in) thick.

3
Rub the ginger paste over the chicken steaks.

4
Whisk the yogurt in a large bowl, add the garlic paste and salt, then rub this mixture into the chicken. Cover and set aside for 1 hour.

5
Preheat a wok (kadhai). Place half the remaining clarified butter or ghee in it. Add the chicken breasts and cook, turning once, until semi-cooked. Remove from the wok and set aside.

6
Add the remaining clarified butter or ghee to the pan and cook the cardamoms and cloves until they crackle. Add the onions and cook until brown.

7
Add the tomatoes, red chilli powder, flour, black pepper and chicken stock. Cook until the sauce becomes rich and thick, stirring occasionally.

8
Place the chicken in the sauce and cook, turning it over gently, for a further 10 minutes. Stir in the mace and saffron. Serve garnished with the fried almonds and fresh coriander.

Serving suggestion
Serve with boiled or pulao rice.

Variation
Use small turkey breasts or steaks in place of chicken breasts.

Kadhai Chicken

A tomato-based chicken delicacy cooked in a wok (kadhai) and flavoured with coriander.

Preparation time: 20 minutes • Cooking time: 45 minutes • Serves: 4

Ingredients

75 ml (5 tbsp) vegetable oil
20 ml (4 tsp) garlic paste
8 whole dried red chillies, roughly ground
5 ml (1 tsp) coriander seeds, roughly ground
1 kg (2 lb 4 oz) tomatoes, skinned and chopped
30 ml (2 tbsp) fresh coriander leaves
45 ml (3 tbsp) root ginger, peeled and chopped
4 green chillies, slit
Salt, to taste
Two 1 kg (2 lb 4 oz) chickens, each cut into 8 pieces
10 ml (2 tsp) garam masala *(page 9)*
Ginger juliennes, to garnish

Method

1
Heat the oil in a wok (kadhai) and cook the garlic paste until brown.

2
Add the ground chillies and coriander seeds and stir-fry for a few seconds.

3
Add the tomatoes and bring to the boil. Add half the coriander leaves and all the ginger, green chillies and salt. Simmer for 5 minutes.

4
Add the chicken and simmer, stirring occasionally, until the sauce thickens and the chicken is cooked and tender.

5
Once the fat rises to the surface, stir in the garam masala and cook for 2 minutes. Garnish with the remaining fresh coriander and ginger juliennes.

Serving suggestion
Serve with naan or chapattis.

Variation
Use turkey or pork in place of chicken.

Saag Murgh

A dish of chicken curried in a spicy spinach purée.

Preparation time: 10 minutes • Cooking time: 45 minutes • Serves: 4

Ingredients

60 ml (4 tbsp) vegetable oil

4 cinnamon sticks

2 bay leaves

40 g (1½ oz) ginger paste (page 7)

40 g (1½ oz) garlic paste (page 7)

200 g (7 oz) onion paste (page 9)

10 ml (2 tsp) red chilli powder

175 g (6 oz) tomatoes, skinned and chopped

350 g (12 oz) cooked spinach, puréed

2.5 ml (½ tsp) corn flour

100 g (3½ oz) butter

One 1 kg (2 lb 4 oz) chicken, skinned and cut into small pieces

Salt, to taste

2.5 ml (½ tsp) white pepper

10 ml (2 tsp) ginger juliennes, to garnish

2.5 ml (½ tsp) ground fenugreek, to garnish

Method

1

Heat the oil in a pan, add the whole spices (cinnamon and bay leaves) and cook over a medium heat until they begin to crackle.

2

Add the ginger, garlic and onion pastes and red chilli powder and cook for 30-60 seconds. Add the tomatoes and cook for 1 minute.

3

Add the spinach purée, stir in the corn flour diluted with 45 ml (3 tbsp) water and cook over a medium heat for 10-15 minutes, stirring occasionally.

4

In a separate pan, heat the butter and cook the chicken until lightly browned all over.

5

Transfer the chicken pieces into the spinach sauce. Add salt and white pepper, cover and simmer over a very low heat for 10-15 minutes or until the chicken is cooked and tender. Serve garnished with ginger juliennes and ground fenugreek.

Serving suggestion

Serve with a mixed leaf salad and boiled or steamed rice.

Variation

Use puréed peas in place of the spinach.

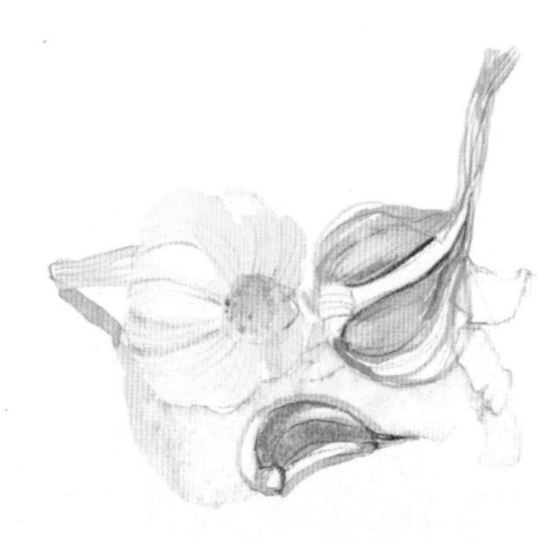

Cardamom-Flavoured Lamb

Cardamom adds a powerfully fragrant quality to this lamb curry.

Preparation time: 20 minutes • Cooking time: 1-1½ hours • Serves: 4

Ingredients

900 g (2 lb) lean lamb, diced
85 g (3 oz) onions, chopped
10 ml (2 tsp) ginger paste *(page 7)*
10 ml (2 tsp) garlic paste *(page 7)*
55 g (2 oz) plain yogurt
55 g (2 oz) unsalted butter
2 green chillies, chopped
Salt, to taste
5 ml (1 tsp) ground cardamom
30 ml (2 tbsp) almond paste
A few drops of rose water
30 ml (2 tbsp) double cream
A pinch of saffron
Ginger juliennes, to garnish

Method

1
Place the lamb into a pan of water and bring to the boil. Drain and wash the pieces of meat.

2
Place the blanched lamb pieces, chopped onions, ginger and garlic pastes, yogurt, butter, chillies, salt and half the ground cardamom in a pan. Bring to the boil and simmer for 1-1½ hours, stirring occasionally, until the lamb is cooked and tender.

3
Add the almond paste and cook gently until the gravy thickens.

4
Add the remaining ground cardamom, rose water and cream, stir to mix and serve.
Sprinkle with saffron crushed in a little water, garnish with ginger juliennes and serve.

Serving suggestion

Serve with Indian bread such as naan or paratha.

Variation

Use beef in place of lamb.

Kid nu Gosht

A flavourful combination of lamb and potatoes cooked in a spicy gravy.

Preparation time: 20 minutes, plus 2 hours marinating time • Cooking time: 1½ hours • Serves: 4

Ingredients

10 ml (2 tsp) ginger paste *(page 7)*

10 ml (2 tsp) garlic paste *(page 7)*

500 g (1 lb 2 oz) stewing lamb, diced

75 ml (5 tbsp) vegetable oil

175 g (6 oz) onions, chopped

2.5 ml (½ tsp) cumin seeds

Salt, to taste

2.5 ml (½ tsp) poppy seeds

85 g (3 oz) cashew nuts

4 green chillies

1 cinnamon stick

4 cloves

2.5 ml (½ tsp) black peppercorns

1 bay leaf

175 g (6 oz) potatoes, diced

250 ml (9 fl oz) coconut milk

Fresh coriander leaves and red and green pepper pieces, to garnish

Method

1
Mix together half the ginger and garlic pastes. Add the lamb, stir to coat all over, then cover and set aside to marinate for 2 hours.

2
In a non-stick pan, heat the oil and cook the onions until lightly browned.

3
Add the remaining ginger and garlic pastes, cumin seeds, salt, poppy seeds, cashew nuts, green chillies and the whole spices (cinnamon, cloves, black peppercorns and bay leaf). Cook for 5 minutes over a moderate heat.

4
Add the lamb and cook for 8-10 minutes. Every few minutes, sprinkle with 15 ml (1 tbsp) water to keep the contents of the pan moist.

5
Add 500 ml (18 fl oz) water and the potatoes. Cover, bring to the boil and simmer for 1-1½ hours, until the lamb is cooked and tender, stirring occasionally.

6
Add the coconut milk, simmer for 1 minute, then remove from the heat. Garnish with the coriander and pepper pieces and serve.

Serving suggestion

Serve hot with steamed rice.

Variation

Use swede or turnip in place of the potatoes.

Rara Meat

Lean lamb cooked until tender in a spicy yogurt sauce.

Preparation time: 20 minutes, plus 1 hour marinating time • Cooking time: 1½ hours • Serves: 4

Ingredients

175 g (6 oz) plain yogurt

Salt, to taste

1 kg (2 lb 4 oz) lean lamb, cut into cubes

150 ml (¼ pint) vegetable oil

2 bay leaves

3 black cardamoms

8 cardamoms

250 g (9 oz) onions, chopped

45 g (3 tbsp) ginger paste *(page 7)*

45 g (3 tbsp) garlic paste *(page 7)*

25 ml (5 tsp) ground coriander

2.5 ml (½ tsp) ground turmeric

5 ml (1 tsp) red chilli powder

175 g (6 oz) tomatoes, skinned and chopped

20 ml (4 tsp) garlic, chopped

20 ml (4 tsp) root ginger, peeled and shredded

10 ml (2 tsp) ground cumin

4 whole red chillies

Chopped fresh coriander and tomato slices, to garnish

Method

1
Whisk together the yogurt and salt. Add the lamb and stir to mix. Cover and set aside to marinate for 1 hour.

2
Heat the oil in a saucepan, add the bay leaves and cardamoms and heat until crackling.

3
Add the onions and cook until lightly browned.

4
Add the ginger and garlic pastes and stir-fry for 4-5 minutes. Stir in the coriander, turmeric and red chilli powder.

5
Add the lamb with the marinade, bring to the boil, then reduce the heat.
Simmer, adding 15 ml (1 tbsp) water occasionally, for about 30 minutes, stirring occasionally.

6
Add the tomatoes, chopped garlic and shredded ginger and stir to mix. Add the cumin and whole red chillies.
Cook over a low heat for 30-45 minutes until the lamb pieces are coated with the sauce and are cooked and tender.
Garnish with coriander and tomato slices and serve.

Serving suggestion

Serve with any Indian bread.

Variation

Use crème fraîche in place of yogurt.

Lamb Rogan Josh

A mild lamb dish originating from Kashmir.

Preparation time: 20 minutes • Cooking time: 1 hour • Serves: 4

Ingredients

1 kg (2 lb 4 oz) lamb chops	*175 g (6 oz) onions, chopped*
Salt, to taste	*10 ml (2 tsp) red chilli powder*
60 ml (4 tbsp) vegetable oil	*2.5 ml (½ tsp) black cumin seeds*
5 ml (1 tsp) sugar	*400 g (14 oz) tomatoes, skinned, seeded and chopped*
10 cloves	*10 ml (2 tsp) ginger paste (page 7)*
3 bay leaves	*200 ml (7 fl oz) lamb stock or water*
8 cardamoms	*5 ml (1 tsp) ground fennel seeds*
2 cinnamon sticks	

Method

1
Clean the lamb chops and remove and discard excess fat. Pat dry with a kitchen paper towel, sprinkle with salt and set aside for 10 minutes.

2
Heat the oil in a pan, add the sugar, cloves, bay leaves, cardamoms and cinnamon sticks and cook for 2-3 minutes.

3
Add the lamb chops and cook over a medium heat until the chops are lightly browned all over.

4
Add the chopped onions and cook until browned.

5
Add the red chilli powder, black cumin seeds, chopped tomatoes and ginger paste and fry until the oil separates from the sauce.

6
Add the stock or water, bring to the boil and cook for about 30 minutes until the chops are tender.

7
Add the ground fennel seeds and cover and simmer for 10 minutes over a low heat. Serve immediately, garnished with a pinch of ground fennel seeds.

Serving suggestion

Serve with steamed rice or Indian bread.

Variation

Use shallots in place of the onions.

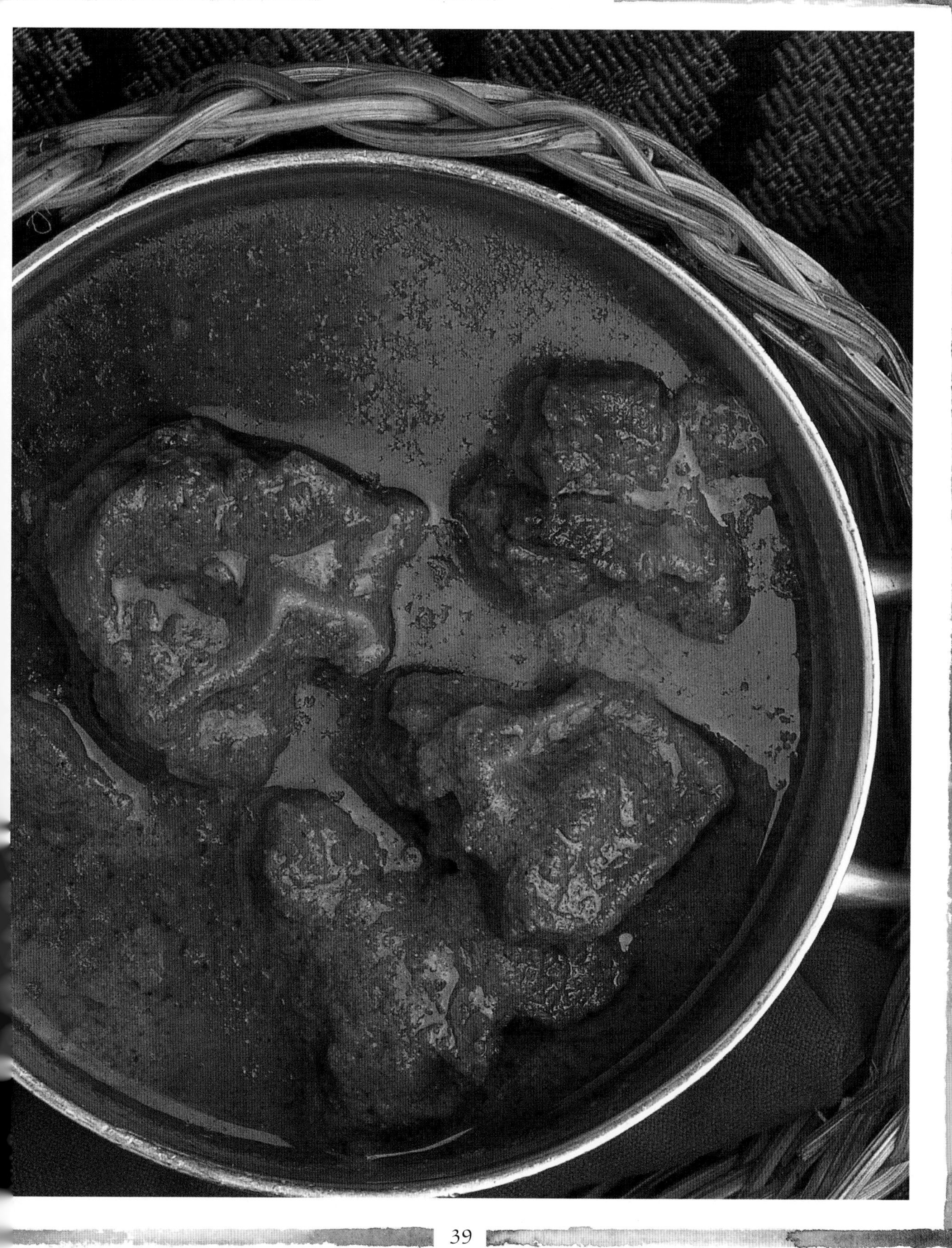

White Mince

The name of this dish is highly descriptive – the minced lamb and sauce are strikingly pale in colour.

Preparation time: 15 minutes, plus 1 hour soaking time • Cooking time: 40 minutes • Serves: 4

Ingredients

15 ml (1 tbsp) blanched almonds

15 ml (1 tbsp) unsalted cashew nuts

15 ml (1 tbsp) poppy seeds

60 ml (4 tbsp) vegetable oil

85 g (3 oz) onions, chopped

15 ml (1 tbsp) garlic, chopped

750 g (1 lb 10 oz) minced lamb

250 g (9 oz) plain yogurt

2.5 ml (1/2 tsp) ground cardamom

5 ml (1 tsp) ground white pepper

4 whole green chillies

Diamond-shaped pieces of red and green pepper, to garnish

Method

1
Soak the almonds in boiling water, then set aside.

2
Soak the cashew nuts and poppy seeds in water for 1 hour. Blend all 3 with a little water to a fine paste in a blender or food processor and set aside.

3
Heat the oil in a wok (kadhai) and cook the onions and garlic over a low heat without letting them brown.

4
Add the mince and cook over a gentle heat until browned all over.

5
Whisk and add the yogurt, ground cardamom, white pepper and whole green chillies and stir to mix. Bring to the boil and simmer gently for about 25 minutes until the mince is cooked and the sauce is reduced by half, stirring occasionally.

6
Remove and discard the green chillies.

7
Add the nut paste and stir well. Simmer for a further 2-3 minutes. Serve immediately, garnished with the pepper pieces.

Serving suggestion

Serve hot with paratha.

Variations

Use pork or beef mince in place of the lamb. Use Brazil nuts in place of the almonds.

Lamb Mughlai

A delicately flavoured lamb curry.

Preparation time: 15 minutes • Cooking time: 50 minutes • Serves: 4

Ingredients

200 ml (7 fl oz) vegetable oil	*100 g (3½ oz) plain yogurt*
4 cinnamon sticks	*1 kg (2 lb 4 oz) lamb chops or cutlets*
6 cardamoms	*300 g (10½ oz) cashew nut paste (page 9)*
8 cloves	*Salt, to taste*
1 bay leaf	*2.5 ml (½ tsp) ground black pepper*
55 g (2 oz) ginger paste (page 7)	*A pinch of saffron*
55 g (2 oz) garlic paste (page 7)	*Chopped fresh coriander and coarsely chopped cashew nuts, to garnish*
55 g (2 oz) green chilli paste (page 9)	

Method

1
Heat the oil in a saucepan. Add the cinnamon, cardamoms, cloves and bay leaf and cook over a medium heat for 30 seconds.

2
Add the ginger, garlic and green chilli pastes and cook for 2 minutes.

3
Add the yogurt and lamb and cook over a low heat for 45 minutes, stirring occasionally, until the lamb is cooked and tender.

4
Add the cashew nut paste, salt, pepper and saffron. Stir briefly, then remove from the heat.
Serve garnished with chopped fresh coriander and cashew nuts.

Serving suggestion
Serve with parathas or naan.

Variation
Use chicken in place of the lamb.

Gosht Shahi Korma

Cubes of lean lamb curried with yogurt, cream and almonds.

Preparation time: 1 hour • Cooking time: 30 minutes • Serves: 4-5

Ingredients

1 kg (2 lb 4 oz) lean boneless lamb
25 g (1 oz) ginger paste (page 7)
25 g (1 oz) garlic paste (page 7)
150 g (5½ oz) clarified butter or ghee
100 g (3½ oz) unsalted butter
2 bay leaves
5 cinnamon sticks
10 cardamoms
150 g (5½ oz) onions, sliced
250 g (9 oz) plain yogurt
50 g (1¾ oz) almond paste
100 ml (3½ fl oz) double cream
6-10 green chillies, seeded and sliced
2.5 ml (½ tsp) ground white pepper
Salt, to taste
2.5 ml (½ tsp) ground cardamom
2.5 ml (½ tsp) ground turmeric, to garnish

Method

1
Wash and dry the lamb and cut into small cubes.

2
Rub the ginger and garlic pastes over the lamb and set aside for 1 hour.

3
Heat the clarified butter or ghee and unsalted butter in a pan. Add the bay leaves, cinnamon sticks and cardamoms and cook until they crackle. Add the onions and cook until soft.

4
Add the cubed lamb and cook over a high heat until the lamb changes colour.

5
Add the yogurt and almond paste and cook over a low heat for a further 25 minutes, or until the lamb cubes are tender. Add the cream, green chillies to taste, ground white pepper, salt and ground cardamom. Heat gently for 2-3 minutes, stirring. Sprinkle with turmeric before serving.

Serving suggestion

Serve with pulao rice and Indian bread.

Variation

Use crème fraîche in place of double cream for a slightly sharper flavour.

Kohe Awadh

A simple yet deliciously aromatic and relatively mild curry.

Preparation time: 15 minutes • Cooking time: 2½-3 hours • Serves: 4

Ingredients

175 g (6 oz) onions, chopped

60 ml (4 tbsp) clarified butter or ghee

1 kg (2 lb 4 oz) lamb meat from the shanks, on the bone, cut into 10 pieces

8 cardamoms

8 cloves

2 cinnamon sticks

2 bay leaves

40 g (1½ oz) ginger paste *(page 7)*

40 g (1½ oz) garlic paste *(page 7)*

Salt, to taste

400 g (14 oz) plain yogurt

5 ml (1 tsp) red chilli powder

5 ml (1 tsp) ground black pepper

1.25 ml (¼ tsp) ground cumin

5 ml (1 tsp) ground mace

1.25 ml (¼ tsp) ground cardamom

5 ml (1 tsp) saffron

2 drops almond essence

15 ml (1 tbsp) milk

10 ml (2 tsp) ginger juliennes, to garnish

Fresh coriander leaves, to garnish

Method

1

Fry the onions in a pan with a little clarified butter or ghee. Remove from the heat, cool slightly, then grind to a paste in a blender or food processor and set aside.

2

In the same pan, heat the remaining clarified butter or ghee and add the lamb, cardamoms, cloves, cinnamon, bay leaves, ginger and garlic pastes and salt. Cover and cook over a low heat for 30 minutes, stirring occasionally. Uncover and stir-fry for a few minutes until the liquid evaporates.

3

Add the yogurt and continue to stir-fry until the liquid evaporates again.

4

Add the red chilli powder, dissolved in 30 ml (2 tbsp) water, and stir for 1 minute. Add the fried onion paste dissolved in 45 ml (3 tbsp) water and continue to fry. Add 15 ml (1 tbsp) water when the liquid evaporates, to ensure that the sauce and the lamb do not burn.

5

Add the pepper and cumin, 1,200 ml (2 pints) water and bring to the boil. Cover tightly, lower the heat and simmer for about 1½ hours, stirring occasionally, until the lamb is cooked and tender.

6

Remove the lamb from the sauce. Strain the sauce, return to the pan and boil the sauce rapidly until it reaches pouring consistency.

7

Add the mace, ground cardamom and the saffron with the almond essence mixed in the milk. Cook for 5 minutes.

8

To serve, pour the sauce over the lamb and garnish with ginger juliennes and fresh coriander leaves.

Serving suggestion

Serve with boiled basmati rice tossed with chopped fresh coriander.

Safed Maas

Safed Maas, literally meaning 'white meat', is an ancient Rajasthani delicacy.

Preparation time: 15 minutes • Cooking time: 1 hour • Serves: 4

Ingredients

1.5 kg (3 lb 5 oz) boneless lamb

Salt, to taste

250 g (9 oz) plain yogurt

5 ml (1 tsp) ground white pepper

55 g (2 oz) almonds, blanched

55 g (2 oz) fresh coconut pieces

150 ml (1/4 pint) vegetable oil

20 ml (4 tsp) ginger juliennes

2.5 ml (1/2 tsp) ground white cardamom

120 ml (4 tsp) double cream

10 ml (2 tsp) lemon juice

5 ml (1 tsp) rose water

6 green chillies, chopped

Method

1

Clean and cut the lamb into 3-cm (1¼-in) cubes. Place in a pan, add the salt and 1.5 litres (2¾ pints) boiling water and boil for 5 minutes. Drain and wash the lamb. Set aside.

2

Mix the yogurt and white pepper together, then set aside.

3

Place the almonds and coconut in a blender or food processor, add 60 ml (4 tbsp) water and blend for 4-5 minutes to form a fine paste.

4

Heat the oil in a pan, add the blanched lamb, the spiced yogurt, ginger juliennes, salt and 850 ml (1½ pints) water. Cover, bring to the boil and simmer for 30-45 minutes, stirring occasionally, until the lamb is cooked and tender and the liquid has almost evaporated.

5

Add the almond and coconut paste and cook for 2 minutes. Add the ground cardamom and stir to mix.

6

Add the cream, lemon juice, rose water and chopped green chillies and stir to mix. Cover the pan tightly and place in a preheated oven at 180°/350°/gas mark 4 for 15 minutes.

7

To serve, transfer the cooked lamb to a shallow dish.

Serving suggestion

Serve with Indian bread or steamed rice.

Variation

Use hazelnuts or cashew nuts in place of almonds.

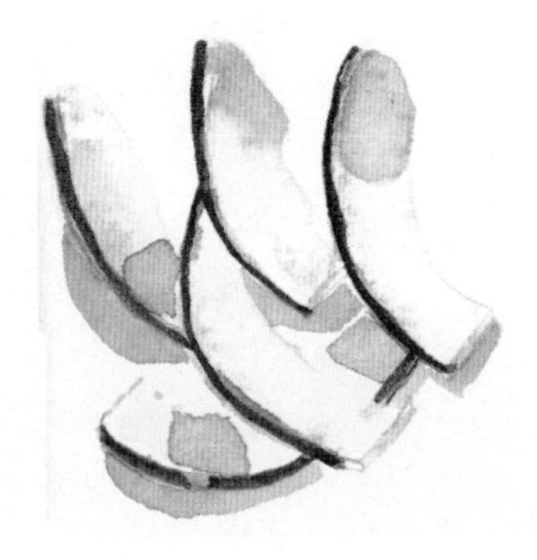

Lamb with Whole Spices

An aromatic lamb dish enhanced with the flavour of crackled whole spices.

Preparation time: 45 minutes • Cooking time: 15 minutes • Serves: 4

Ingredients

120 ml (8 tbsp) vegetable oil
250 g (9 oz) onions, sliced
25 g (1 oz) root ginger
45 ml (3 tbsp) garlic cloves
15 ml (1 tbsp) poppy seeds
2 black cardamoms
1 cinnamon stick
1 bay leaf
6 cloves
250 g (9 oz) plain yogurt
750 g (1 lb 10 oz) lamb escalopes 5 x 10 cm (2 x 4 in)
5 ml (1 tsp) red chilli powder
5 ml (1 tsp) garam masala *(page 9)*
2.5 ml (1/2 tsp) ground cardamom
2.5 ml (1/2 tsp) ground black pepper
5 ml (1 tsp) chopped fresh coriander, to garnish

Method

1
Heat half the oil in a wok (kadhai) and cook half the onions until golden brown. Remove from the pan and set aside.

2
Peel and chop the ginger and garlic. Mix with the browned and raw onions and poppy seeds, then blend in a food processor or blender to a fine paste with 30 ml (2 tbsp) water.

3
Heat the remaining oil in the wok (kadhai) and heat the black cardamoms, cinnamon, bay leaf and cloves until they crackle. Add the blended paste and cook for 3-4 minutes.

4
Add the yogurt and cook for 4-5 minutes. Add the lamb and cook for a further 3-4 minutes until the fat rises to the surface, stirring occasionally.

5
Transfer to a casserole dish. Add 120 ml (8 tbsp) water and stir to mix.

6
Sprinkle the red chilli powder, garam masala, ground cardamom and black pepper over the top. Cover and cook in a preheated oven at 200°/400°/gas mark 6 for 15 minutes. Garnish with fresh coriander and serve.

Serving suggestion

Serve hot with sliced onion rings, quartered tomatoes, shredded crisp lettuce and naan.

Variation

Use sesame seeds in place of poppy seeds.

Nahari Gosht

This curried lamb was a favourite dish of the Nawabs of Lucknow.

Preparation time: 15 minutes • Cooking time: 1 hour 10 minutes • Serves: 4

Ingredients

1 kg (2 lb 4 oz) lamb on the bone (any cut)

150 ml (1/4 pint) mustard oil

250 g (9 oz) onions, sliced

250 g (9 oz) onions, chopped

10 cardamoms

10 cloves

4 cinnamon sticks

20 black peppercorns

2 bay leaves

20 ml (4 tsp) ground coriander

8 whole red chillies

10 ml (2 tsp) ground turmeric

5 ml (1 tsp) ginger paste *(page 7)*

5 ml (1 tsp) garlic paste *(page 7)*

Salt, to taste

200 g (7 oz) plain yogurt

5 ml (1 tsp) plain flour

5 ml (1 tsp) gram flour

10 ml (2 tsp) garam masala *(page 9)*

5 ml (1 tsp) ground fennel

10 ml (1 tsp) lemon juice

15 ml (1 tbsp) almond essence

A pinch of saffron

2.5 ml (1/2 tsp) ground mace

15 ml (1 tbsp) chopped fresh coriander, to garnish

Method

1
Clean and cut the lamb into small pieces with the bone.

2
Heat 100 ml (3½ fl oz) of the oil in a wok (kadhai), add the sliced onions and cook over a medium heat until golden brown.

3
Add the lamb, chopped onions, cardamoms, cloves, cinnamon, black peppercorns and bay leaves and cook until the liquid evaporates, stirring occasionally.

4
Add the ground coriander, red chillies, turmeric, ginger and garlic pastes and salt and cook until the oil separates from the mixture.

5
Add the yogurt, bring to the boil, reduce the heat to medium and cook for 10 minutes.

6
Add 1 litre (1¾ pints) water and bring to the boil again. Cover and simmer for about 30 minutes, stirring occasionally, until the lamb is tender. Remove the meat from the sauce, cover and set aside.

7
Heat the remaining oil in a pan, add the flour and gram flour and cook over a low heat, stirring constantly, until lightly browned. Add the sauce and stir until thickened.

8
Pour the thickened sauce through a sieve, return to the pan and bring to the boil.

9
Add the lamb, garam masala, ground fennel, lemon juice, almond essence, saffron and mace and stir to mix. Garnish with fresh coriander and serve.

Serving suggestion

Serve with Indian bread such as naan or paratha.

Variations

Use beef in place of lamb. Use crème fraîche in place of yogurt.

Potato and Paneer Dumplings in Curry

Deliciously satisfying fried dumplings in a tomato-based sauce. Serve with Indian bread and a green salad.

Preparation time: 25 minutes • Cooking time: 50 minutes • Serves: 6

Ingredients

For the dumplings	For the curry
500 g (1 lb 2 oz) paneer (page 7), grated	*40 g (1½ oz) cashew nuts or almonds, finely chopped*
3-4 potatoes, boiled and mashed	*15 ml (1 tbsp) root ginger, peeled and finely chopped*
45 ml (3 tbsp) fresh coriander, chopped	*2 green chillies, chopped*
45 ml (3 tbsp) mixed nuts, finely chopped	*7.5 ml (1½ tsp) ground coriander*
2.5 ml (½ tsp) ground turmeric	*5 ml (1 tsp) ground cumin*
A pinch of ground asafoetida	*2.5 ml (½ tsp) ground turmeric*
15 ml (1 tbsp) root ginger, peeled and finely shredded	*75 ml (5 tbsp) clarified butter or ghee*
1-2 green chillies, seeded and finely chopped	*5 ml (1 tsp) cumin seeds*
2.5 ml (½ tsp) dry mango powder	*1 cinnamon stick*
5 ml (1 tsp) lemon juice	*4 cloves*
7.5 ml (1½ tsp) salt	*600 g (1 lb 5 oz) tomatoes, skinned and finely chopped*
30 ml (2 tbsp) cornflour	*Salt, to taste*
Vegetable oil, for frying	*Double cream, to garnish*

Method

1

For the dumplings, knead the grated paneer until it is of a smooth and creamy texture. Add the mashed potatoes, coriander, mixed nuts, turmeric, asafoetida, ginger, green chillies, dry mango powder, lemon juice, salt and cornflour and knead until the ingredients are thoroughly mixed.

2

Lightly oil your hands and divide the mixture into 12 portions. Roll each portion into a ball. Place all the balls on a tray lined with plastic wrap, cover and set aside.

3

Heat oil in a wok (kadhai) to 180°C/350°F. Slide in a few balls at a time and fry until golden brown all over.

4

Remove from the oil, drain excess oil on kitchen paper towels and set aside.

5

For the curry, place the nuts, ginger, green chillies, ground coriander, cumin and turmeric in a blender or food processor and blend with enough water to make a smooth paste. Set aside.

6

Heat the clarified butter or ghee in a heavy-based pan over a moderate heat. Stir-fry the cumin seeds, cinnamon stick and cloves for 10-15 seconds.

7

Stir in half the tomatoes and the prepared paste and cook until the liquid from the tomatoes evaporates and the oil separates.

8

Add the remaining tomatoes, 250 ml (9 fl oz) water and salt. Cover the pan and simmer for 10-15 minutes, or until the curry has thickened slightly.

9

Carefully stir in the dumplings and bring the curry to the boil.

10

Spoon the dumplings into a serving dish, pour the curry over the top and garnish with cream. Serve.

Kadhi

A tangy yogurt and gram flour-based curry sauce with puffy, deep-fried dumplings.

Preparation time: 25 minutes • Cooking time: 45 minutes • Serves: 4

Ingredients

350 g (12 oz) plain yogurt

Salt, to taste

5 ml (1 tsp) red chilli powder

5 ml (1 tsp) ground turmeric

125 g (4½ oz) gram flour

A pinch of bicarbonate of soda

2.5 ml (½ tsp) carom seeds

5 green chillies, chopped

Vegetable oil, for deep-frying

60 ml (4 tbsp) groundnut oil

150 g (5½ oz) potatoes, cut into rounds about 5 mm (¼ in) thick

150 g (5½ oz) onions, cut into 5-mm (¼-in) thick slices

2.5 ml (½ tsp) cumin seeds

1.25 ml (¼ tsp) mustard seeds

1.25 ml (¼ tsp) fenugreek seeds

4 whole red chillies

Whole red and green chillies, to garnish

Method

1
Whisk the yogurt, salt, red chilli powder, turmeric and half the gram flour together in a bowl. Set aside.

2
Sift the remaining gram flour and bicarbonate of soda together, add the carom seeds and add enough water to make a thick batter. Beat well. Add the green chillies.

3
Heat enough oil in a wok (kadhai) to deep-fry. Drop large spoonfuls of the batter in the oil to make 4-mm (1½-in) puffy dumplings. Fry until golden brown on both sides. Remove and set aside.

4
Heat 45 ml (3 tbsp) groundnut oil in a pan, add the yogurt mixture and 700 ml (1¼ pints) water. Bring to the boil, reduce to a low heat and simmer for 8-10 minutes, stirring constantly, to prevent the yogurt curdling.

5
Add the potatoes and onions and cook until the potatoes are cooked and tender.

7
Add the dumplings and simmer for 3 minutes.

8
Heat the remaining 15 ml (1 tbsp) oil in a small frying pan. Add the cumin, mustard and fenugreek seeds and cook until the cumin crackles. Add the whole red chillies and stir. Pour over the simmering hot curry. Serve garnished with the red and green chillies.

Serving suggestion

Spoon the dumplings and sauce into a bowl and serve with boiled rice.

Variation

Use sweet potatoes in place of standard potatoes.

Plantain Kofta

Plantains, or 'green bananas' as they are often called, form the basis of these spicy dumplings (koftas) which are served in a thick, aromatic sauce.

Preparation time: 45 minutes • Cooking time: 45 minutes • Serves: 4

Ingredients

450 g (1 lb) green bananas
55 g (2 oz) onions, finely chopped
15 ml (1 tbsp) root ginger, peeled and finely chopped
20 ml (4 tsp) fresh coriander, chopped
6 green chillies, finely chopped
2.5 ml (1/2 tsp) ground white pepper
Salt, to taste
Vegetable oil, for deep-frying
6 cardamoms
4 cloves
1 cinnamon stick
55 g (2 oz) onions, roughly chopped
15 ml (1 tbsp) ginger paste *(page 7)*
15 ml (1 tbsp) garlic paste *(page 7)*
175 g (6 oz) tomatoes, skinned and chopped
5 ml (1 tsp) red chilli powder
60 ml (4 tbsp) double cream
5 ml (1 tsp) honey
A pinch of ground mace
Ginger juliennes and chopped fresh coriander, to garnish

Method

1
Place the green bananas in a pan, cover with boiling water and boil for 30 minutes. Cool, peel and mash.

2
Mix in the finely chopped onion and ginger, coriander, green chillies, white pepper and salt. Divide the mixture into 15 portions and roll into balls between your palms. Deep-dry in a wok (kadhai) over a low heat until golden brown all over. Set aside and keep warm.

3
Remove excess oil from the wok (kadhai) reserving 60 ml (4 tbsp). Heat the oil and the cardamoms, cloves and cinnamon and cook until they begin to crackle. Add the roughly chopped onions and cook until transparent. Add the ginger and garlic pastes and cook until the onions turn brown.

4
Purée the tomatoes in a blender or food processor.

5
Add the tomato purée, red chilli powder and salt to the wok (kadhai) and stir-fry until the oil rises to the surface.

6
Add 400 ml (14 fl oz) water. Bring to the boil, remove from the heat and strain through a sieve into another pan.

7
Place the pan on the heat and bring the sauce to the boil. Add the cream. Remove from the heat and add the honey.

8
Arrange the koftas in an ovenproof casserole dish. Pour the sauce over, sprinkle with ground mace and tightly cover the dish.

9
Bake in a preheated oven at 200°C/400°F/gas mark 6 for 10 minutes. Serve immediately garnished with ginger juliennes and fresh coriander.

Serving suggestion
Serve with boiled rice or paratha.

Variation
Use crème fraîche in place of cream.

Kadhai Paneer

A chilli-hot, semi-dry and colourful vegetarian curry, cooked in a wok (kadhai).

Preparation time: 15 minutes • Cooking time: 15 minutes • Serves: 4

Ingredients

600 g (1 lb 5 oz) paneer *(page 7)*

40 g (1½ oz) green pepper

14 whole dried red chillies

10 ml (2 tsp) coriander seeds

40 g (1½ oz) vegetable oil

40 g (1½ oz) onions, chopped

15 ml (1 tbsp) ginger juliennes

150 g (5½ oz) tomato purée

Salt, to taste

5 ml (1 tsp) ground fenugreek

10 ml (2 tsp) garam masala *(page 9)*

10 ml (2 tsp) ground coriander

10 ml (2 tsp) ground black pepper

15 ml (1 tbsp) chopped fresh coriander, to garnish

Method

1

Cut the paneer into fingers and set aside. Cut the green pepper in half, remove the seeds and make juliennes or cut into small, even squares. Set aside.

2

Pound the red chillies and coriander seeds with a pestle and mortar to form a powder.

3

Heat the oil in a wok (kadhai) and cook the onions and green pepper over a medium heat for 2 minutes.

4

Add the pounded spices and ⅔ of the ginger juliennes and cook for 1 minute, stirring. Add the tomato purée and salt, bring to the boil and simmer until the oil separates from the sauce.

5

Add the paneer and cook gently for 2-3 minutes, stirring.

6

Sprinkle with fenugreek, garam masala, ground coriander and black pepper and stir to mix.

7

To serve, garnish with fresh coriander and the remaining ginger juliennes.

Serving suggestion

Serve with paratha and a mixed salad or raita (plain yogurt mixed with a little chopped cucumber, onion, chopped fresh coriander and ground cumin).

Variation

Use a red or yellow pepper in place of the green pepper.

Shahi Paneer

Fingers of paneer (see page 7) served in a yogurt and cream sauce.

Preparation time: 20 minutes • Cooking time: 25-30 minutes • Serves: 4

Ingredients

75 ml (5 tbsp) vegetable oil
6 cloves
2 bay leaves
3 cinnamon sticks
6 cardamoms
200 g (7 oz) onion paste (page 9)
40 g (1½ oz) ginger paste (page 7)
40 g (1½ oz) garlic paste ((page 7)
10 ml (2 tsp) red chilli powder
5 ml (1 tsp) ground turmeric
5 ml (1 tsp) ground coriander
10 ml (2 tsp) cashew nut paste (page 9)
Salt, to taste
A few drops of red food colouring
175 g (6 oz) plain yogurt
10 ml (2 tsp) sugar
120 ml (8 tbsp) double cream
10 ml (2 tsp) garam masala (page 9)
2.5 ml (½ tsp) ground cardamom
2.5 ml (½ tsp) ground mace
A few drops of almond essence
A pinch of saffron, dissolved in 15 ml (1 tbsp) milk
1 kg (2 lb 4 oz) paneer (page 9), cut into fingers
Chopped fresh coriander, to garnish

Method

1
Heat the oil in a pan, add the cloves, bay leaves, cinnamon sticks and cardamoms and cook over a medium heat until they begin to crackle. Add the onion paste and stir-fry for 2-3 minutes.

2
Stir in the ginger and garlic pastes, red chilli powder, turmeric, ground coriander, cashew nut paste, salt and food colouring.

3
Add the yogurt, 100 ml (3½ fl oz) warm water and sugar. Bring to the boil, then simmer until the oil separates. Remove the pan from the heat.

4
Allow the curry to cool, then remove the whole spices and discard. Blend the curry to a smooth consistency in a blender or food processor. Return to the rinsed-out pan.

5
Reheat the curry, then stir in the cream, garam masala, ground cardamom, mace, almond essence and saffron mixture.

6
Add the paneer fingers and cook for a further 5 minutes, stirring occasionally.

7
Serve hot, garnished with fresh coriander.

Serving suggestion

Serve with any dry vegetable dish and parathas.

Variation

Use tofu or Quorn in place of the paneer.

Prawn Curry

A traditional prawn curry from southern India. Seafood in India is readily available in the south since most states have a long coastline.

Preparation time: 20 minutes • Cooking time: 30 minutes • Serves: 4

Ingredients

1 kg (2 lb 4 oz) prawns
85 g (3 oz) fresh coconut, grated
60 ml (4 tbsp) groundnut oil
5 ml (1 tsp) mustard seeds
200 g (7 oz) onions, chopped
20 ml (4 tsp) garlic paste *(page 7)*
10 ml (2 tsp) ginger paste *(page 7)*
10 ml (2 tsp) ground coriander
10 ml (2 tsp) red chilli powder
2.5 ml (1/2 tsp) ground turmeric
Salt, to taste
300 g (10 1/2 oz) tomatoes, skinned and chopped
10 curry leaves
Chopped fresh coriander and ginger juliennes, to garnish

Method

1
Shell and devein the prawns, then wash and pat them dry.

2
Put the coconut in a blender or food processor with 60 ml (4 tbsp) water and blend to make a fine paste.

3
Heat the oil in a pan and heat the mustard seeds until they crackle. Add the onions and cook over a medium heat until transparent.

4
Add the garlic and ginger pastes. Stir and cook until all the liquid has evaporated.

5
Add the ground coriander, red chilli powder, turmeric and salt. Stir to mix.

6
Add the tomatoes and cook until soft and pulpy, stirring occasionally.

7
Reduce the heat to low and add the prepared coconut paste and curry leaves. Stir for 2 minutes.

8
Add the prawns and approximately 400 ml (14 fl oz) water. Bring to the boil, reduce the heat and simmer for about 10 minutes, stirring occasionally, until the prawns are cooked. Transfer to a bowl and garnish with ginger juliennes and fresh coriander.

Serving suggestion
Serve hot with boiled rice.

Baked Prawns with Pomegranate

An exotic prawn dish, also known as Jhinga Dum Anari.

Preparation time: 25 minutes, plus 30 minutes marinating time • Cooking time: 10-12 minutes • Serves: 4

Ingredients

800 g (1 lb 12 oz) jumbo prawns
30 ml (2 tbsp) malt vinegar
Salt, to taste
2.5 ml (1/2 tsp) yellow or red chilli powder
10 ml (2 tsp) ginger paste *(page 7)*
10 ml (2 tsp) garlic paste *(page 7)*
125 g (4 1/2 oz) fresh peas
25 g (1 oz) Cheddar cheese, grated, plus extra
55 g (2 oz) pickled onions, chopped
10 ml (2 tsp) fresh coriander, chopped
5 ml (1 tsp) root ginger, peeled and finely chopped
2.5 ml (1/2 tsp) cumin seeds
30 ml (2 tbsp) lemon juice
2.5 ml (1/2 tsp) white pepper
45 ml (3 tbsp) tomato ketchup
250 g (9 oz) fresh pomegranate seeds
Ginger juliennes and split green chillies, to garnish

Method

1
Remove the heads from the prawns and discard. Slit and devein the prawns, then wash and pat them dry.

2
Mix the malt vinegar, salt, yellow or red chilli powder and ginger and garlic pastes together.
Add the prawns, mix well and marinate for 30 minutes.

3
Place each prawn on a separate 25-cm (10-in) square of greased aluminium foil.

4
Boil, drain and crush the peas with a rolling pin. Mix in the grated cheese, onion, coriander, ginger, cumin, lemon juice, white pepper, tomato ketchup and pomegranate seeds.

5
Top each prawn with some of this mixture. Grate a little extra cheese on each and wrap up in the foil.

6
Place the parcels on a baking tray and bake in a preheated oven at 180°C/350°F/gas mark 4 for 10-12 minutes.
Serve hot garnished with ginger juliennes and green chillies.

Serving suggestion
Serve with any Indian bread, such as naan.

Variation
Use baby broad beans in place of peas.

Fish in Tomato Sauce

A delicate dish of sole fillets, which literally melts in the mouth.

Preparation time: 20 minutes, plus 30 minutes marinating time • Cooking time: 35 minutes • Serves: 4

Ingredients

15 ml (1 tbsp) ginger paste *(page 7)*

10 ml (2 tsp) garlic paste *(page 7)*

Salt, to taste

30 ml (2 tbsp) lemon juice

10 ml (2 tsp) red chilli powder

600 g (1 lb 5 oz) sole fillets

10 ml (2 tsp) fresh coconut, grated

10 ml (2 tsp) sunflower seeds

10 ml (2 tsp) unsalted cashew nuts

120 ml (8 tbsp) vegetable oil

25 g (1 oz) garlic, peeled and chopped

300 g (10½ oz) tomatoes, skinned and chopped

5 ml (1 tsp) garam masala *(page 9)*

75 ml (5 tbsp) double cream

10 ml (2 tsp) chopped fresh coriander, to garnish

Method

1
Mix together the ginger and garlic pastes, salt, lemon juice and half the red chilli powder in a bowl. Add the fish and stir to mix. Cover and set aside to marinate for 30 minutes.

2
Meanwhile, blend the coconut, sunflower seeds and cashew nuts in a blender or food processor until smooth.

3
Heat the oil in a pan. Add the fish and cook gently for 10 minutes, turning occasionally. Remove, set aside and keep hot.

4
In the remaining hot oil, cook the peeled garlic until golden brown. Add the tomatoes and stir-fry until they are soft and pulpy.

5
Stir in the remaining red chilli powder and cook for 5 minutes.

6
Strain the sauce through a sieve and return to the pan.

7
Add the coconut, sunflower seed and cashew nut paste and stir for 2-3 minutes.

8
Add the garam masala and the fried fish. Reserve 30 ml (2 tbsp) cream for garnishing and add the rest to the sauce. Simmer for 2-3 minutes, stirring. Garnish with fresh coriander and the remaining cream. Serve hot.

Serving suggestion

Serve with sliced fresh tomatoes, cucumber slices and lemon wedges accompanied by boiled or steamed rice.

Variation

Use cod or haddock fillets in place of sole.

Prawn Balchao

This is a favourite Goan dish which can be stored up to 2 days in the refrigerator before serving. In fact, its tangy flavour is at its best after a day or so.

Preparation time: 25 minutes • Cooking time: 25 minutes • Serves: 4

Ingredients

1 kg (2 lb 4 oz) small prawns
2.5 ml (1/2 tsp) black peppercorns
12 cardamoms
4 cinnamon sticks
15 cloves
2.5 ml (1/2 tsp) cumin seeds
15 whole red chillies
150 ml (1/4 pint) malt vinegar
150 ml (1/4 pint) groundnut oil
175 g (6 oz) onions, chopped
15 ml (1 tbsp) ginger paste *(page 7)*
30 ml (2 tbsp) garlic paste *(page 7)*
125 g (4 1/2 oz) tomatoes, skinned and chopped
12 curry leaves
25 g (1 oz) sugar

Method

1
Shell and devein the prawns, then wash and pat them dry. Set aside.

2
Blend the peppercorns, cardamoms, cinnamon, cloves, cumin and red chillies with the vinegar in a blender or food processor until smooth. Set aside.

3
Heat the oil in a wok (kadhai) and deep-fry the prawns until golden brown. Remove from the oil and set aside. Keep hot.

4
Add the onions to the hot oil and cook until golden brown.

5
Add the ginger and garlic pastes and stir-fry for 1 minute.

6
Add the tomatoes and the blended paste and stir-fry for 2-3 minutes.

7
Add the fried prawns, curry leaves and sugar and cook for 5-10 minutes until the prawns are tender. Serve.

Serving suggestion
Serve hot with steamed rice or any Indian bread.

Variation
Use leeks in place of the onions.

Fish Curry

This dish of small, fresh sea fish in a thick, brown curry topped with a liberal sprinkling of whole red chillies is very popular in southern India.

Preparation time: 45 minutes • Cooking time: 30 minutes • Serves: 4

Ingredients

30 ml (2 tbsp) lemon juice
900 g (2 lb) small whole fresh fish, such as sardines
Vegetable oil, for frying
75 ml (5 tbsp) groundnut oil
5 ml (1 tsp) mustard seeds
2.5 ml (½ tsp) fenugreek seeds
2 cardamoms
1 cinnamon stick
2 cloves
6 whole red chillies
125 g (4½ oz) fresh coconut, grated
25 g (1 oz) tamarind, soaked in 100 ml (3½ fl oz) water
85 g (3 oz) onions, sliced
125 g (4½ oz) tomatoes, skinned and chopped
5 ml (1 tsp) ground turmeric
Salt, to taste
10 curry leaves, plus extra for garnishing

Method

1
Sprinkle the lemon juice over the fish and set aside for 30 minutes. Wash with fresh water, squeeze lightly and pat dry. Fry the fish lightly in oil and set aside. Keep hot.

2
In a small pan, heat 15 ml (1 tbsp) groundnut oil. Add the mustard seeds, fenugreek seeds, cardamoms, cinnamon, cloves and whole red chillies and cook gently for 2 minutes. Set aside to cool, then blend to a smooth paste in a blender or food processor with the grated coconut.

3
Mash the soaked tamarind with your fingers, then squeeze out and discard the pulp. Reserve the juices and set aside.

4
Heat the remaining groundnut oil in a pan and cook the onions until brown. Add the tomatoes and turmeric and stir-fry for 4-5 minutes. Add the tamarind extract and bring to the boil, reduce the heat and simmer for a further 5 minutes.

5
Add the coconut paste to the sauce and cook until the sauce thickens. Add the salt and curry leaves.

6
Gently add the fried fish to the curry and simmer for 5 minutes. Garnish with curry leaves.

Serving suggestion
Serve hot with boiled rice.

Variation
Use prawns or mixed seafood in place of fish.

Mahi Musallam

A whole large fish baked in a cashew nut and fenugreek sauce.

Preparation time: 20 minutes, plus 1 hour marinating time • Cooking time: 1 hour • Serves: 4

Ingredients

2 kg (4 lb 8 oz) whole river or sea fish, e.g. trout, salmon, cod or haddock

200 ml (7 fl oz) vegetable oil

200 g (7 oz) onion paste (page 9)

55 g (2 oz) ginger paste (page 7)

55 g (2 oz) garlic paste (page 7)

100 g (3½ oz) cashew nut paste (page 9)

15 ml (1 tbsp) ground coriander

10 ml (2 tsp) red chilli powder

10 ml (2 tsp) ground turmeric

Salt, to taste

175 g (6 oz) plain yogurt

5 ml (1 tsp) ground fenugreek

15 ml (1 tbsp) garam masala (page 9)

5 drops almond essence

15 ml (1 tbsp) lemon juice

30 ml (2 tbsp) melted butter, to garnish

Onion rings and lemon halves, to garnish

For the marinade paste

20 ml (4 tsp) garlic paste (page 7)

20 ml (4 tsp) ginger paste (page 7)

15 ml (1 tbsp) lemon juice

5 ml (1 tsp) red chilli powder

Salt, to taste

Method

1
Clean, wash and wipe the fish thoroughly and set aside.

2
Mix all the ingredients for the marinade in a bowl. Prick the fish all over with a sharp knife and rub the marinade all over and set aside for 1 hour.

3
Heat the oil in a pan to smoking point. Arrange the fish in a baking dish. Baste the fish with the hot oil until the fish is partly cooked.

4
Add the onion, ginger, garlic and cashew nut pastes to the oil left in the pan and stir to mix. Add the ground coriander, red chilli powder, turmeric and salt and mix well.

5
Add the yogurt, bring the mixture to the boil, reduce to a medium heat and stir until the oil separates from the mixture.

6
Add 300 ml (½ pint) hot water and bring it slowly to the boil. Add the ground fenugreek, garam masala and almond essence.

7
Preheat the oven to 150°C/300°F/gas mark 2. Pour the hot sauce over the fish and bake for 30-40 minutes, basting the fish occasionally with the sauce.

8
To serve, remove the fish from the baking dish and arrange it carefully in a shallow dish. Strain the sauce and stir in the lemon juice. Pour the sauce over the fish and garnish with melted butter, onion rings and lemon halves.

Serving suggestion

Serve with plain boiled or steamed rice or Indian bread.

Variation

Use crème fraîche in place of yogurt.

Vegetable Korma

An interesting combination of vegetables, mildly spiced and laced with fresh coconut.

Preparation time: 25 minutes • Cooking time: 30 minutes • Serves: 4

Ingredients

175 g (6 oz) fresh coconut, grated

2 green chillies, chopped

30 ml (2 tbsp) onions, chopped

5 m (1 tsp) root ginger, peeled and chopped

2.5 ml (1/2 tsp) ground turmeric

10 ml (2 tsp) fresh coriander, chopped

10 ml (2 tsp) fennel seeds

1 cinnamon stick

3 cloves

6 cardamoms

10 ml (2 tsp) poppy seeds

100 g (3 1/2 oz) green beans, chopped

100 g (3 1/2 oz) carrots, siced

100 g (3 1/2 oz) kohlrabi, diced

100 g (3 1/2 oz) peas, shelled

100 g (3 1/2 oz) potatoes, diced

100 g (3 1/2 oz) tomatoes, skinned and chopped

2 bay leaves

Salt, to taste

30 ml (2 tbsp) clarified butter or ghee

Whole unsalted cashew nuts, to garnish

Method

1
Place the coconut, green chillies, onions, ginger, turmeric and fresh coriander in a blender or food processor and blend to a fine paste. Set aside.

2
On a hot griddle or in a heavy-based frying pan, dry-fry the fennel seeds, cinnamon, cloves, cardamoms and poppy seeds. Cool, then blend to a fine powder in a blender or food processor.

3
Place the vegetables in a pan with just enough water to cover. Add the bay leaves and salt and bring to the boil. Boil for 15-20 minutes until the vegetables are cooked.

4
Once the vegetables are tender and the water has evaporated, add the coconut-onion paste. Stir-fry for 2-3 minutes.

5
Add the ground spice mixture and clarified butter or ghee. Stir well and cook for 5 minutes, stirring. Sprinkle with cashew nuts before serving.

Serving suggestion

Serve with any Indian bread.

Variation

Garnish with blanched, slivered almonds in place of the cashew nuts.

Raseele Kum-Kum

Baked whole tomatoes stuffed with a lemon and mint-flavoured mushroom mixture in a creamy tomato-based sauce.

Preparation time: 15 minutes • Cooking time: 1 hour • Serves: 4

Ingredients

15 firm, round tomatoes
30 ml (2 tbsp) vegetable oil
25 g (1 oz) onions, chopped
15 ml (1 tbsp) garlic, chopped
100 g (3½ oz) tomato pulp, fresh or canned
5 ml (1 tsp) green chillies, finely chopped
500 g (1 lb 2 oz) mushrooms, chopped
Salt, to taste
10 ml (2 tsp) garam masala *(page 9)*
10 ml (2 tsp) fresh mint leaves, chopped
10 ml (2 tsp) lemon juice
2.5 ml (½ tsp) ground black cumin, roasted or dry-fried
10 ml (2 tsp) fresh coriander, chopped
25 ml (5 tsp) vegetable oil
2.5 ml (½ tsp) cardamoms
1 bay leaf
25 g (1 oz) onions, sliced
10 ml (2 tsp) garlic
300 g (10½ oz) tomatoes, skinned and chopped
Salt, to taste
60 ml (4 tbsp) double cream
2.5 ml (½ tsp) ground mace

Method

1
Slice the tops off the tomatoes and scoop out and discard the flesh. Set the tomato shells and tops to one side.

2
Heat the oil in a pan and cook the onions, garlic and tomato pulp over a medium heat until the moisture is completely evaporated and the oil separates from the sauce.

3
Add the green chillies and chopped mushrooms, stir and cook over a high heat for 10-15 minutes until the water evaporates.

4
Add the salt, garam masala, chopped mint leaves, lemon juice, cumin and half the fresh coriander. Set aside to cool.

5
Fill each tomato with the mushroom mixture and cover with a tomato top. Place the stuffed tomatoes on a greased baking tray and bake at 180°/350°/gas mark 4 for 15-20 minutes.

6
Meanwhile, make the sauce. Heat the oil in a pan. Cook the cardamoms, bay leaf, onions, garlic and tomatoes for 5 minutes. Add 400 ml (14 fl oz) water and salt and cook for about 30 minutes, stirring occasionally.

7
Strain through a fine sieve. Transfer the sauce to a saucepan and bring to the boil. Remove the pan from the heat and add the cream and ground mace.

8
To serve, pour the sauce over the baked tomatoes and sprinkle with the remaining fresh coriander before serving.

Serving suggestion

Serve on a bed of rice with a mixed side salad.

Variations

Use courgettes in place of mushrooms and fresh basil in place of mint.

Subz Jalfrezi

A chilli-hot, dry curry of mixed vegetables – quick and easy to prepare and cook.

Preparation time: 15 minutes • Cooking time: 15 minutes • Serves: 4

Ingredients

75 ml (5 tbsp) vegetable oil
5 cardamoms
5 whole red chillies
100 g (3½ oz) onions, chopped
10 ml (2 tsp) ground turmeric
10 ml (2 tsp) red chilli powder
5 ml (1 tsp) ground white pepper
2.5 ml (½ tsp) ground cumin
1 green capsicum
150 g (5½ oz) potatoes, diced
150 g (5½ oz) carrots, sliced
150 g (5½ oz) button onions
150 g (5½ oz) cauliflower, cut into small florets
150 g (5½ oz) tomatoes, skinned and chopped
150 g (5½ oz) button mushrooms
5 ml (1 tsp) sugar
30 ml (2 tbsp) white wine vinegar
15 ml (1 tbsp) garam masala *(page 9)*
Salt, to taste

To garnish

15 ml (1 tbsp) green chillies, sliced
15 ml (1 tbsp) fresh coriander, chopped
Green pepper, cut into rings

Method

1
Heat the oil in a pan, add the cardamoms and whole red chillies and cook over a medium heat until they begin to crackle.

2
Add the chopped onions and cook until lightly browned.

3
Add the turmeric, red chilli powder, white pepper and cumin and cook for 30 seconds.

4
Cut the green capsicum into long strips and add to the pan with the potatoes, carrots, button onions, cauliflower, tomatoes and button mushrooms and cook for a further 30 seconds over a high heat.

5
Add the sugar, vinegar, garam masala and salt and cook for 30 seconds.

6
Cover and cook for 6 minutes, stirring occasionally, until the vegetables are cooked and tender. Garnish with green chillies, fresh coriander and green capsicum rings and serve.

Serving suggestion

Serve on a bed of boiled or steamed rice.

Variation

Use a selection of vegetables of your choice, such as shallots, baby sweetcorn, swede, sweet potatoes and broccoli.

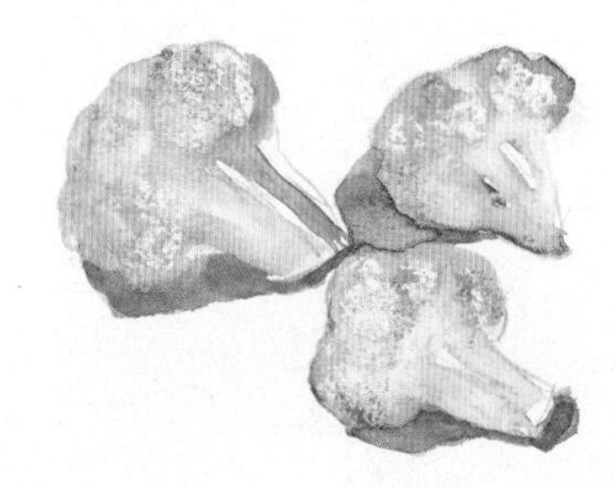

Lotus Root in Exotic Curry

The lotus root's creamy flesh has a flavour similar to fresh coconut.
If fresh lotus root is unavailable, use the canned variety.

Preparation time: 10 minutes • Cooking time: 30 minutes • Serves: 4

Ingredients

800 g (1 lb 12 oz) lotus root
250 ml (9 fl oz) mustard oil
2 cloves
2 green cardamoms
30 ml (2 tbsp) ground fennel
2.5 ml (½ tsp) ground cumin
2.5 ml (½ tsp) ground cinnamon
5 ml (1 tsp) ground black cardamom
5 ml (1 tsp) salt
1.5 kg (3 lb 5 oz) plain yogurt

Method

1
Scrape away and discard the skin of the lotus root. Cut into 4-cm (1½-in) long pieces, discarding the ends. Wash well under cold running water and drain.

2
Heat the mustard oil in a wok (kadhai) and deep-fry the pieces of lotus root for about 10 minutes until they are partly cooked. Drain and set aside.

3
Add 100 ml (3½ fl oz) water and the lotus root to the wok and bring to the boil. Add all the spices and salt and mix in the yogurt. Cook over a medium heat until the curry thickens and the lotus root is cooked and tender, stirring frequently.

4
Transfer to a serving dish and serve hot.

Serving suggestion
Serve with plain boiled rice.

Variation
Use okra in place of the lotus root.

Minced Peas and Potatoes

A substantial, mildly spiced vegetable curry.

Preparation time: 15 minutes • Cooking time: 30 minutes • Serves 4-6

Ingredients

1-2 green chillies, chopped

4-cm (1½-in) piece root ginger, peeled and chopped

400 g (14 oz) tomatoes, skinned and chopped

75 ml (5 tbsp) clarified butter or ghee

300 g (10½ oz) peas, minced

5 ml (1 tsp) cumin seeds

6 cloves, ground

10 ml (2 tsp) ground cinnamon

5 ml (1 tsp) ground black pepper

15 ml (1 tbsp) ground coriander

5 ml (1 tsp) ground turmeric

2.5 ml (½ tsp) red chilli powder

5-6 small potatoes, diced

Salt, to taste

15 ml (1 tbsp) garam masala *(page 9)*

30 ml (2 tbsp) chopped fresh coriander, to garnish

Method

1
Place the green chillies, ginger and tomatoes in a blender or food processor and blend until smooth. Set aside.

2
Heat the 60 ml (4 tbsp) of the clarified butter or ghee in a wok (kadhai) and brown the minced peas until the oil separates. Set aside.

3
Heat the remaining butter or ghee in a pan and add the cumin seeds and fry for a few seconds. Add the browned pea paste, cloves, cinnamon, black pepper, ground coriander, turmeric and red chilli powder and cook for a few minutes, stirring.

4
Stir in the green chilli, ginger and tomato purée and bring to the boil. Add the diced potatoes and cook for 10-15 minutes until the potatoes are cooked and tender.

5
Season with salt and garam masala, garnish with fresh coriander and serve hot.

Serving suggestion

Serve with naan or paratha.

Variation

Use sweet potatoes in place of the standard potatoes.

Cook's tip

A quick and easy way to skin tomatoes is to cut a small cross in the base of each tomato using a sharp knife. Place the tomatoes in a bowl and cover them with boiling water. Leave for 30 seconds, then transfer to a bowl of cold water using a slotted spoon. Remove the tomatoes from the water and peel off the skins. Remove the seeds, if you like, by cutting the tomatoes in half and scooping out and discarding the seeds.

Curried Eggplant

Baby eggplant cooked until tender in an aromatic sauce. If baby eggplant are unavailable, use full-sized eggplant and cut into thick rounds.

Preparation time: 20 minutes • Cooking time: 30 minutes • Serves: 4

Ingredients

5 ml (1 tsp) coriander seeds

10 ml (2 tsp) cumin seeds

10 ml (2 tsp) poppy seeds

10 ml (2 tsp) sesame seeds

35 g (1¼ oz) desiccated coconut

15 ml (1 tbsp) tamarind

400 g (14 oz) baby eggplant

120 ml (8 tbsp) mustard oil

10 ml (2 tsp) ginger paste (page 7)

10 ml (2 tsp) garlic paste (page 7)

5 ml (1 tsp) ground turmeric

10 ml (2 tsp) red chilli powder

10 curry leaves

Salt, to taste

Slit green chillies, ginger juliennes and tomato quarters, to garnish

Method

1
Dry-fry the coriander, cumin, poppy and sesame seeds on a hot griddle or in a heavy-based frying pan. Allow to cool, then crush. Dry-fry the coconut separately on the griddle or in the frying pan and set aside.

2
Wash and soak the tamarind in 250 ml (9 fl oz) warm water. After 10 minutes, mash well, squeeze and discard the pulp. Set the juices aside.

3
Slit the eggplant along about ¾ of their length.

4
Heat the oil in a wok (kadhai) and fry the eggplant lightly. Remove from the pan and set aside.

5
In the same oil, brown the ginger and garlic pastes, ground spices, turmeric, red chilli powder, curry leaves and coconut.

6
Cook gently, stirring occasionally and adding a little water if the sauce begins to burn.

7
Add the eggplant, 450 ml (16 fl oz) water and salt and mix well. Simmer for 10 minutes.

8
Add the tamarind juice through a sieve and simmer until the sauce thickens. Garnish with green chillies, ginger juliennes and tomato quarters and serve.

Serving suggestion
Serve with plain boiled rice or Indian bread.

Variation
Use zuchinni in place of eggplant.

Fried Okra

A delicious coconut-flavoured fried okra curry from southern India.

Preparation time: 15 minutes • Cooking time: 45 minutes • Serves: 4

Ingredients

800 g (1 lb 12 oz) okra
Groundnut oil, for deep-frying
15 ml (1 tbsp) cashew nuts
85 g (3 oz) fresh coconut, grated
60 ml (4 tbsp) coconut milk
2.5 ml (½ tsp) cumin seeds
5 ml (1 tsp) mustard seeds
20 ml (4 tsp) split red lentils
3 whole red chillies
10 curry leaves
125 g (4½ oz) onions, chopped
250 g (9 oz) tomatoes, skinned and chopped
5 ml (1 tsp) red chilli powder
2.5 ml (½ tsp) ground turmeric
15 ml (1 tbsp) ground coriander
Salt, to taste
125 g (4½ oz) plain yogurt
Slit green chillies and tomato quarters, to garnish

Method

1
Wash and dry the okra, then cut it into 2.5-cm (1-in) pieces.

2
Heat the groundnut oil in a wok (kadhai) and deep-fry the okra over a medium heat for about 5-6 minutes until crisp. Drain and reserve the oil and okra separately.

3
Place the cashew nuts and the coconut in a blender or food processor, add the coconut milk and blend to make a fine paste.

4
Heat 75 ml (5 tbsp) of the reserved oil, add the cumin and mustard seeds, lentils, whole red chillies and the curry leaves. Cook over a medium heat until the seeds begin to crackle.

5
Add the onions and cook until golden brown.

6
Stir in the tomatoes, then add the red chilli powder, turmeric, coriander and salt. Cook until the fat rises to the surface, stirring continuously.

7
Reduce the heat, add the coconut paste and cook for a further 2 minutes, stirring.

8
Remove the pan from the heat and add the yogurt. Stir in 400 ml (14 fl oz) water. Return the pan to the heat and bring to the boil. Simmer for 15 minutes.

9
Add the deep-fried okra and cook gently for 10 minutes. To serve, transfer to a shallow dish and garnish with the green chillies and tomato quarters.

Serving suggestion

Serve with boiled or steamed rice.

Variation

Use baby courgettes or baby sweetcorn in place of okra.

Mattar Makhana Korma

Green peas and puffed lotus seeds are cooked in a green chilli and yogurt sauce.

Preparation time: 15 minutes • Cooking time: 25 minutes • Serves: 4

Ingredients

600 g (1 lb 5 oz) peas	*40 g (1½ oz) garlic paste (page 7)*
200 g (7 oz) puffed lotus seeds	*25 g (1 oz) green chilli paste (page 9)*
60 ml (4 tbsp) vegetable oil	*100 g (3½ oz) cashew nut paste (page 9)*
10 cloves	*200 g (7 oz) plain yogurt*
3 cinnamon sticks	*Salt, to taste*
1 bay leaf	*2.5 ml (½ tsp) ground white pepper*
8 cardamoms	*60 ml (4 tbsp) double cream*
55 g (2 oz) onions, chopped	*10 ml (2 tsp) butter*
40 g (1½ oz) ginger paste (page 7)	*Lemon wedges, cucumber slices and onion rings, to garnish*

Method

1
Parboil the peas and puffed lotus seeds in boiling water for 5 minutes. Drain and set aside.

2
Heat the oil in a pan. Add the cloves, cinnamon sticks, bay leaf and cardamoms and cook for 30 seconds. Add the chopped onions and cook until golden.

3
Add the ginger, garlic, green chilli and cashew nut pastes and cook until the oil separates from the sauce.

4
Add the yogurt and cook over a low heat for 5 minutes. Add the peas, lotus seeds, salt and white pepper. Cover and cook over a low heat for 5 minutes, stirring occasionally.

5
Stir in the cream and keep hot. In a separate pan, lightly fry the ginger juliennes in the butter. Serve garnished with lemon wedges, cucumber slices and onion rings.

Serving suggestion
Serve with steamed or boiled rice.

Variation
Use green beans or broad beans in place of peas.

Dum Aloo Bhojpuri

Deep-fried potato shells are stuffed with a grated potato and mixed spice filling and served with a yogurt-based curry in this unusual and delicious vegetable dish.

Preparation time: 25 minutes • Cooking time: 25 minutes • Serves: 4

Ingredients

15 ml (1 tbsp) clarified butter or ghee
85 g (3 oz) onions, grated
30 ml (2 tbsp) ginger paste (page 7)
30 ml (2 tbsp) garlic paste (page 7)
200 g (7 oz) potatoes, boiled and grated
10 ml (2 tsp) red chilli powder
5 ml (1 tsp) ground turmeric
10 ml (2 tsp) garam masala (page 9)
15 ml (1 tbsp) lemon juice
Salt, to taste

600 g (1 lb 5 oz) small, round potatoes
Vegetable oil, for deep-frying
45 ml (3 tbsp) vegetable oil
1 bay leaf
2 cinnamon sticks
6 cloves
6 cardamoms
2.5 ml (1/2 tsp) black cumin seeds
150 g (5 1/2 oz) plain yogurt
Ginger juliennes, to garnish

Method

1
Heat the clarified butter or ghee in a pan, add half each of the grated onion, ginger and garlic pastes and fry for 4-5 minutes. Add the grated potatoes, half the red chilli powder, turmeric and garam masala. Season with half the lemon juice and salt and set aside.

2
Boil and peel the small potatoes. Scoop out the centres and deep-fry the shells until slightly crisp. Remove from the oil and drain well.

3
Fill each potato shell with the prepared potato filling. Cover and set aside.

4
Heat the 45 ml (3 tbsp) oil in a pan over a medium heat. Add the bay leaf, cinnamon sticks, cloves, cardamoms and black cumin seeds and fry until they begin to crackle.

5
Mix in the remaining onions and ginger and garlic pastes and stir-fry for 2-3 minutes.

6
Add the remaining turmeric and red chilli powder and stir-fry over a medium heat for 5-6 minutes. Stir in the yogurt. Cook until the liquid evaporates, stirring frequently. Sprinkle with the remaining garam masala and season with salt.

7
Arrange the stuffed potatoes in the pan. Sprinkle with the remaining lemon juice, cover and cook for 3-4 minutes over a very low heat.

8
Serve hot garnished with ginger juliennes.

Serving suggestion

Serve with boiled or steamed rice or parathas.

Variation

Use cooked, grated carrots or swede in place of the grated potatoes.

Curried Spinach Balls

These spinach balls, or koftas, are deep-fried and served in a mild and creamy curry sauce.

Preparation time: 20 minutes • Cooking time: 30 minutes • Serves: 4

Ingredients

For the koftas
175 g (6 oz) spinach
15 ml (1 tbsp) poppy seeds
30 ml (2 tbsp) unsalted cashew nuts, coarsely chopped
2.5 ml (1/2 tsp) ground coriander
2.5 ml (1/2 tsp) ground cumin
2.5 ml (1/2 tsp) red chilli powder
Salt, to taste
Vegetable oil, for deep-frying

For the sauce
30 ml (2 tbsp) vegetable oil
2.5 ml (1/2 tsp) cumin seeds
1 medium onion, chopped
5 ml (1 tsp) ginger paste (page 7)
5 ml (1 tsp) garlic paste (page 7)
30 ml (2 tbsp) cashew nut paste (page 9)
2.5 ml (1/2 tsp) ground turmeric
5 ml (1 tsp) red chilli powder
Salt, to taste
250 g (9 oz) tomatoes, skinned and chopped
Chopped fresh coriander and cream, to garnish

Method

1
To make the koftas, clean, wash and boil the spinach leaves for 4 minutes. Cool, then squeeze out as much water from the spinach as possible and finely chop. Set aside.

2
Grind the poppy seeds and cashew nuts to a paste with a pestle and mortar or a blender.

3
Mix together all the remaining ingredients for the koftas, except the oil, with the paste and spinach.

4
Divide the mixture into 8 portions. Form balls by rolling each portion between the palms of your hands. Heat the oil in a wok (kadhai) and deep-fry the balls until golden brown. Drain, set aside and keep warm.

5
For the sauce, heat 30 ml (2 tbsp) oil in a wok (kadhai). Add the cumin seeds and cook for 30 seconds. Add the chopped onion and cook until browned.

6
Add the ginger, garlic and cashew nut pastes, turmeric, red chilli powder and salt and stir-fry for 2-3 minutes.

7
Add the chopped tomatoes and stir-fry for a further 8-10 minutes. Add 120 ml (8 tbsp) water, bring to the boil and simmer for 5 minutes.

8
Before serving, add the koftas to the sauce and simmer for 5 minutes, until heated through. To serve, pour into a serving bowl and garnish with fresh coriander and cream.

Serving suggestion

Serve with Indian bread such as naan or paratha.

Variation

Use walnuts or hazelnuts in place of cashew nuts.

Index